# BEHIND THE LEGEND

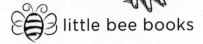
little bee books

An imprint of Bonnier Publishing USA

251 Park Avenue South, New York, NY 10010

Copyright © 2017 by Bonnier Publishing USA

Cover illustration by Victor Rivas

All rights reserved, including the right of reproduction in whole or in part in any form.

LITTLE BEE BOOKS is a trademark of Bonnier Publishing USA, and associated colophon is a trademark of Bonnier Publishing USA.

Manufactured in the United States LB 0817

Names: Peabody, Erin, author. | Tejido, Jomike, illustrator.
Title: Zombies / Erin Peabody; illustrated by Jomike Tejido.
Description: New York, NY: Little Bee Books, 2017. | Series: Behind the legend
Identifiers: LCCN 2017003439 | Subjects: LCSH: Zombies—Juvenile literature.
BISAC: JUVENILE NONFICTION / Social Science / Folklore & Mythology. |
JUVENILE NONFICTION / People & Places / General. | JUVENILE NONFICTION /
Science & Nature / Discoveries. | Classification: LCC GR581.P43 2017
DDC 398.21—dc23 | LC record available at https://lccn.loc.gov/2017003439

ISBN 978-1-4998-0461-4 (hardcover)
First Edition 10 9 8 7 6 5 4 3 2 1
ISBN 978-1-4998-0460-7 (paperback)
First Edition 10 9 8 7 6 5 4 3 2 1

littlebeebooks.com
bonnierpublishingusa.com

# ZOMBIES

by Erin Peabody

art by Jomike Tejido

little bee books

# CONTENTS

# MEET THE MONSTER

"Forgive the zombies; it's not their fault your brains are so delicious."—Simon Swatman, *Plants vs. Zombies: Official Guide to Protecting Your Brains*

**Z**ombies are the ultimate monsters. Half-rotten corpses brought back to life, these terrifying creatures shuffle around sheathed in translucent gray-green skin that's battered, bruised, and bloodied. Instead of bright, shining windows to the soul, their eye sockets feature two ghoulish, milk-colored orbs.

Zombies embody death, and smell like it, too (the most common comparison being spoiled meat . . . "Eeeww!"). Their unintelligible moans and groans are unlike any other sound made by human or beast.

But perhaps most frightening of all is the zombie's unwavering focus. Despite having no mind, the vacant-eyed creeper seems to possess a boundless determination in hunting for victims.

Even after it's been fought off, escaped from, or mutilated in some gory way, the zombie—like a boomerang or rubber ball—ALWAYS bounces back. It strikes again and again. And again. A zombie's terror never ends.

Undoubtedly, you've encountered these deadly shufflers in books, cartoons, movies, games, and more. Looking like everyday people (except that they're zoned out, partially decayed, dressed in tattered clothes, and hungry for brains!), zombies have invaded our culture and consciousness. Some fear that zombies threaten plague-like epidemics, full-blown apocalypse, and most disturbing of all, the theft of our very souls!

But consider this: Our fear of the zombie is fairly laughable—downright pitiful even—in comparison to the *real* zombies of the past.

However, before we venture down this deep, dark path in world history, let's explore a little more about the so-called "undead," "reanimated," and "living dead."

Mortal minds beware: These creepy inquiries are sure to raise your spirits!

CHAPTER ONE

# GHOULISH STORIES SCRAWLED IN CLAY

"I will knock down the Gates of the Netherworld . . .
and will let the dead go up to eat the living!"—The goddess
Ishtar in the ancient book *The Epic of Gilgamesh*

Despite their wild successes, authors like Stephen King, J. K. Rowling, and R. L. Stine are hardly the first to spin spooky yarns about ghouls and the raised dead. In fact, people's interest in the undead goes back thousands of years! (Apparently, we've always been a little warped!)

We can find evidence of this curious, albeit weird, obsession with the dead in skimming through the vast record of literature, the earliest of which dates back to around 4,000 years ago. And believe it or not, a startling scene featuring hungry dead people shows up in the oldest-known work ever written: *The Epic of Gilgamesh*, written in 2100 BCE!

This collection of mythical stories, originally scrawled on clay tablets, was written in Mesopotamia, an ancient region comprised of modern-day Iraq, Kuwait, and parts of Syria. And while the tales certainly lack the bloodshed of current zombie-inspired dramas, they do feature their share of violent battles, angered gods, avenging souls, and perhaps the most painful of life's episodes (as you may be able to attest to), unrequited love.

# (REALLY) BAD ROMANCE

In one part of *Gilgamesh*, Ishtar, the goddess of love, tries to woo Gilgamesh, the king of Uruk. The confident and alluring Ishtar seeks to beguile the vain Gilgamesh for the sake of a good challenge (or maybe because of his long, lustrous hair). But when Gilgamesh rejects her, and Ishtar's powerful father, a ruling god, refuses to mount a retaliation on her behalf, Ishtar does more than just pout.

A drama queen with the universe at her fingertips, Ishtar threatens to use her divine powers to upend the world. If she doesn't get what she wants, she says, she'll release the dead and have them feast on the living. Her father quickly gives in to her heinous threat and grants her access to the muscular Bull of Heaven. Ishtar quickly unleashes the mighty beast on Gilgamesh and his friend, Enkidu.

The two men survive and defeat the monster, but they *never* forget Ishtar's blistering vengeance.

Belief in the undead or walking dead was once widespread across the world. In Western Europe, especially during the twelfth and thirteenth centuries, many people believed a person could rise from the grave and would do so with the intent to carry out a mischievous or evil deed. A wandering corpse was called a *revenant*, a word that's related to the French verb *revenir*, which means "to come back."

One old popular story in England tells of two peasants, presumably dead and buried, who were later seen walking through a village, carrying their wooden coffins above their heads. Another tells of a man who rose from the dead to guard a treasure. And, in one unusually upbeat medieval tale, a woman returns from her grave to return a favor: to cook dinner for the people who tended to her burial!

# KINDRED CREEPS

The terms *ghoul* and *zombie* are often used interchangeably. And in many ways, little more than a ghostly veil differentiates them. In pop culture, both are considered evil beings with a perverse penchant for eating the dead, particularly human flesh—Uuck!!!

That should be enough to generally cast them in the same creepy category, but horror experts say that there are some technical differences between the two. For instance, ghouls, unlike zombies, are generally not the dead brought back to life. They are simply greedy, gluttonous (and even comical) shape-shifters that skulk in graveyards hunting for their next meal. Ghouls can also be clever, plotting, and diabolical compared to their mindless zombie counterparts.

# "GHOULS" IN THE DESERT

Again, Americans can't claim to be the inventors of these horrific corpse-crunchers! Nope, ghouls were first documented in a set of ancient tales written between the eighth and thirteenth centuries! This famous collection of stories, originating in the Middle East and South Asia, is known as the *One Thousand and One Nights* (aka *Arabian Nights*). And in one of these stories, the protagonist is faced with a horde of ravenous "ghūls." (Not *ghouls*, the European version of the word, which came later—but *ghūls*, the Arabic one.)

The basic plot behind *One Thousand and One Nights* involves a new bride, Scheherazade, and her desperate struggle to survive. The king she's been forced to marry is so jealous and vindictive that he's murdered several of his previous wives.

To distract him and preserve her own life, Scheherazade cleverly begins spinning tale upon riveting tale—cliff-hanger-type stories she weaves for a total of 1,001 nights.

One of these stories is *The History of Gherib and His Brother Agib*, in which exiled prince Gherib must battle his brother, Agib, plus a clan of flesh-eating ghouls, for a spot on the throne. You'll be happy to know he accomplishes these feats with relative ease.

# DON'T STEAL MY CHI!

Most living-dead legends and stories feature reanimated corpses that shuffle, roam, lurch, or march. But what about corpses that hop? Yes, bounce up and down! Well, in Chinese folklore, the undead are known to do just *that*!

Called *jiangshi*, these not-quite-dead beings possess inflexible or rigid bodies. (In fact, *jiang* is a Chinese word meaning "hard" or "stiff.") Basically, in a state of rigor mortis, the inflexible jiangshi cannot move any muscles or limbs. And as such, they can only hop.

According to the myths about these leaping deadweights, which originated at least three hundred years ago during China's Qing dynasty, jiangshi are most active at night. They search for victims (presumably peppy, bubbly types!) from which to steal life-giving energy. In Chinese philosophy, this vital energy is known as *qi* or *chi*.

Jiangshi have leapt right into modern pop culture, too, inspiring a whole genre of horror and action flicks that are most popular in Asia.

As you can see, ghūls or ghouls (and other forms of the living dead) are ancient and quite worldly. Almost every culture on the globe has its own version of the living dead. But what about the most reviled of revived corpses, zombies? These out-of-the-grave creepers seem to be everywhere right now, yet their deep, dark history remains largely under wraps. In the next chapter, however, we'll lay open this tomb of zombie secrets and learn the real, haunting truth about these monsters.

## CHAPTER TWO

# THE REAL ZOMBI: A TRUE HORROR

"Zombification had always struck me as the most horrible of fates." —Scientist Wade Davis in his book, *The Serpent and the Rainbow*

* This chapter contains material about slavery that may be difficult to read. Please consult a trusted grown-up (parent, teacher, or librarian) before reading.

According to our imagination, the dead have all kinds of ways of reinventing themselves. We've been entertaining the gruesome possibilities for centuries now. But the most popular comeback kid from the graveyard, at least as of late, has got to be the zombie. These incredibly disgusting, decomposing-before-your-very-eyes creeps seem to be everywhere right now—books, comics, movies, games, television, and much more.

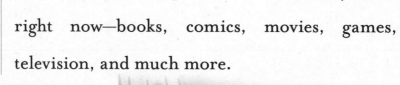

We laugh and joke about zombies with the same reckless abandon a fictitious modern zombie might display in tearing off our limbs. But zombie experts and fans (you!) have a responsibility to know the truth behind the sacred and scary zombi. For that, let's take a dark path back in time to the early 1600s, specifically to the humid sugarcane fields of historic Haiti. . . .

# HORRORS FROM HISTORY

For any newcomers to the area, it should have been a beautiful island. Called Saint-Domingue (today's Haiti), the island was situated in the turquoise Caribbean Sea. It was lush and green, with rolling valleys and mountains that poked above a covering of mist. Warm, moist ocean breezes fluttered through the fronds of palm trees, wafting the exotic sweet perfume of plumeria and other flowers. Bizarre, colorful birds cooed, swarming trees heavy with fruits and berries.

But strangers to this land didn't find a paradise. Far from it, Saint-Domingue would become their prison, a place where humanity revealed its most hideous self. That's because the newcomers being delivered to this island in the 1500s, 1600s, and 1700s were black slaves. They'd been brutally ripped away from their homes in West Africa and forced onto ships. Locked in filthy, rat-infested holds, or the bowels, of a ship, they were forced to endure the nauseating journey across the Atlantic Ocean to Haiti.

Life only got worse once they shuffled off the boats. Immediately, slaves were forced into harsh physical labor. The Spanish and French who'd colonized the island discovered that its lush soils and climate were ideal for growing sugarcane, a highly coveted crop in the fifteenth and seventeenth centuries. Many Europeans at the time were willing to pay a pretty penny for a spoonful of sugar in their tea. Specialty crops like sugar, coffee, and indigo were very lucrative for trading around the world and represented big money to plantation owners in the Caribbean and American South. The obstacle with these crops, though, was that they required a lot of hard work to produce them. This problem, the greedy plantation owners figured, could be solved with slaves.

# WORKED TO DEATH

First, the wealthy French owners enslaved Haiti's indigenous people, the Taíno, as laborers—at least those who were still alive at the time of French rule. You see, these natives—who once flourished across the Caribbean and were the first to welcome Christopher Columbus to the New World in 1492—were dying by the *hundreds* of thousands. Like numerous other indigenous peoples across the globe upon meeting newcomers, the Taíno perished because they lacked immunity (the body's

natural defenses) to smallpox and other foreign diseases that were brought to the islands by colonists. So swift and deadly were these illnesses that an estimated three *million* Taíno (about 85 percent of the entire population) had already died by the early 1500s! Those who remained were harshly enslaved, leading to a near extinction of the entire Taíno people. The French colonists, hungry for free manpower to keep their sugarcane operations buzzing, set their sights on Africa.

# LIKE BARBECUE? THEN SAY THANKS TO THE TAÍNO

Pronounced "tie-no," the Taíno were the Caribbean's first inhabitants. They once prospered across today's island nations of Haiti, the Dominican Republic, Jamaica, Cuba, Puerto Rico, and the Virgin Islands and Bahamas. Successful farmers, these island dwellers grew sweet potatoes, maize (a more ancient form of corn), beans, and other crops.

They were also inventive. The Taíno designed and built ocean-hardy canoes that could hold up to 100 paddlers. They made effective medicines from wild plants. And for sport, they played games with a ball they crafted from rubber plants.

These first peoples of the Caribbean were also generous, an observation not lost on Christopher Columbus, who noted upon meeting the Taíno in 1492 in the Bahamas, "They will give all that they do possess for anything that is given to them, exchanging things even for bits of broken crockery." Of course, Columbus also fatefully remarked that they would make "good servants."

Ultimately, disease, warfare, and slavery would cause the Taíno culture to nearly collapse. Fortunately, their descendants alive today are working hard to sustain their culture's traditions. And if you've ever had an occasion to enjoy a zesty *barbeque* (Who hasn't?!) or paddle across a lake in a *canoe* (You should!), you can pay homage to those early islanders, too. That's because the Taíno invented these words, along with other illustrious ones such as *hammock*, *tobacco*, and *hurricane*.

The work performed by Haiti's slaves was grueling. They labored from early dawn until late at night. A typical day's food for them consisted of a couple of potatoes or a bowl of thick manioc porridge. (Manioc is a potato-like root vegetable.) Slaves also slept in cramped, overcrowded huts.

A visitor to the island in 1790 noted hearing terrible sounds upon waking up one morning. Immediately after hearing the rooster's cries, the man heard "the cracking of the whip, the choking of screams, the deafening groans of the Negroes who experience the beginning of the day only to curse it. . . ."

If slaves were caught sneaking a taste of sugarcane while they worked, they were forced to wear tin muzzles over their mouths. If they didn't work quickly enough, they were punished, beaten, or sprayed with boiling sugarcane. And the victims who tried to flee this terror often suffered a horrific consequence: slave owners would cut the runaways' hamstring muscles, leaving the slaves crippled or severely disabled. As a result of such violent brutality, many slaves perished or took their own lives.

While this history is difficult to read, it's necessary to convey just how frightening and horrible the slave experience in historic Haiti was. These people, stripped of their loved ones, their farms, their jobs, their hopes and dreams, were—as they saw it—reduced to zombis. They had been whipped thoroughly, both physically and psychologically. Their spirit had been savagely stolen from them.

The slaves were treated harshly—forced to work in the sugarcane fields until they practically collapsed. But even more difficult, perhaps, was that slaves were forbidden to socialize among one another: to talk, communicate, or even share a quick exchange with a friend or loved one. Camaraderie that might have helped lift their spirits was totally prohibited by the French colonial leaders in power.

Rules dictating what the slaves could and could not do were detailed in a 1685 French document called the *Code Noir* (or Black Code), an edict of King Louis XIV that was imposed across all of France's colonies. The Code forbade the slaves to gather, except for religious purposes. Even then, the slaves could only worship as Catholics and were often baptized in this religion against their will. The Code also spelled out barbaric penalties for such offenses as runaway slaves, who, if caught, were to have their ears cut off and be branded with a French fleur-de-lis symbol.

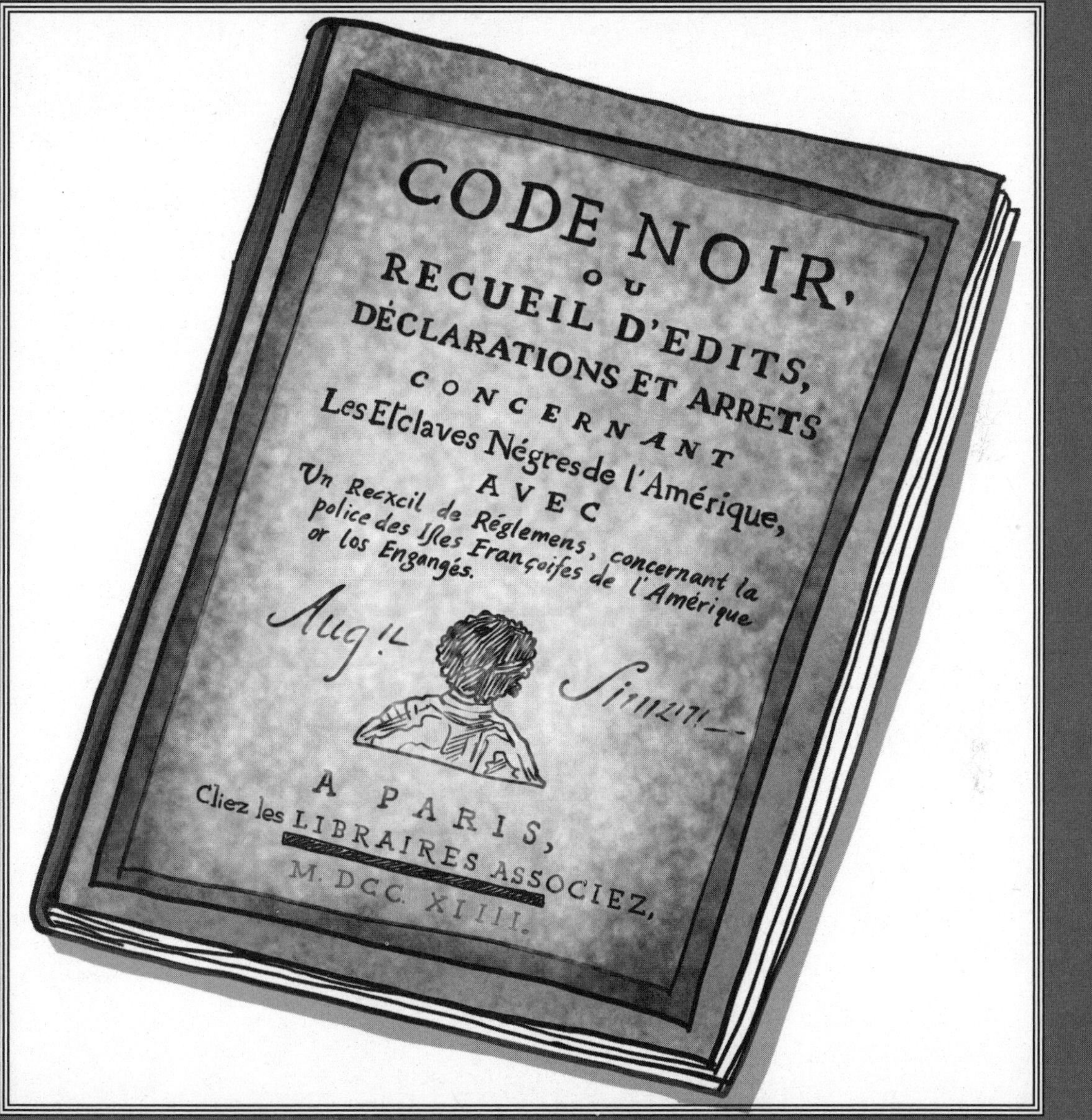
CODE NOIR,
OU
RECUEIL D'EDITS,
DÉCLARATIONS ET ARRETS
CONCERNANT
Les Etclaves Négres de l'Amérique,
AVEC
Un Recxcil de Réglemens, concernant la
police des Isles Françoifes de l'Amérique
or los Engangés.
A PARIS,
Cliez les LIBRAIRES ASSOCIEZ,
M. DCC. XIIII.

Even more rules, the Police Rulings of 1758 and 1777, applied specifically to Saint-Domingue and forbade slaves from gathering at all "during the night or day." The penalty for breaking this rule was grave: death. Regardless, many slaves were determined to keep their ties with friends and loved ones. Many paid a horrible price for coordinating clandestine meetings. Others who dared to swap bits of conversation in the dark of night managed to survive. Their brazen courage ultimately helped the slaves pave a path to freedom.

While beaten and battered, the slaves were
not broken. As people often do in times of great
difficulty, enslaved Haitians drew upon their
faith. Risking their lives, some successfully
escaped to the jungles. There, friends gathered
in the shadows. In whispers, secret plots were
hatched.

A will to survive and persist had bubbled over. The slaves had been mightily and tragically oppressed, but they would not stand for such abuse much longer.

## CHAPTER THREE

# VODOU: IT'S NOT WHAT YOU THINK

"The ant never dies under the weight of a sack of sugar."
—Creole proverb that means the weak may
suffer, but they will persevere

The Haitian slaves' collective spirituality, called Vodou, was a powerful and energizing force. The slaves in Saint-Domingue came from a variety of African tribes, but most originated from West Africa. Their system of beliefs—including ideas about god, what happens when a person dies, and the numerous active spirits that permeate daily life—was derived largely from this West African region.

The Vodou religion helped sustain the slaves when they were forced into servitude on the fearful, strange island of Saint-Domingue, thousands of miles from their homeland. One spirit of great value to them was likely Ogou Badagris, the Vodou (and also Nigerian) god of war. This spirit warrior inspired the slaves to take up arms and fight for their lives.

# UPRISING

At the same time, other cries for liberty were sending ripples across the Atlantic Ocean to Haiti. The French Revolution, which broke out in France in 1789, and its Declaration of the Rights of Man and of the Citizen, spurred enslaved people around the world to question the barbaric institution of slavery. The French humanitarian group known as *Amis des Noirs* (Friends of the Blacks) was particularly vocal and vigilant about ending slavery.

ADRESSE
A L'ASSEMBLÉE NATIONALE,
POUR
L'ABOLITION DE LA TRAITE DES NOIRS.
Par la Socilu des Amis des Noirs di Paris.

This major revolution in Europe, coupled with the rising strength and resolve of the Haitian people themselves, ultimately helped fuel a slave rebellion on Saint-Domingue of epic proportions in 1791. The main operatives in this revolt were runaway slaves who the colonial leaders called "maroons." (The word *maroon* is derived from the Spanish word *cimarron* and means a domesticated animal that's reverted to a wild state.)

The slaves revolted—in some cases, violently—and the colonial powers waged their own bloody response. For instance, French officials released 1,500 dogs on the island to hunt for renegade slaves, who, if caught, were swiftly brutalized. By the end of the rebellion, numerous lives on both sides were lost, but the slaves managed to finally throw off the yoke of the oppressive French colonial power. Astonishingly, these freedom fighters, with no military training at all, defeated Napoleon Bonaparte's world-class army of soldiers. And in 1804, the colony formerly known as Saint-Domingue was given the new name of Haiti, which, according to the nation's indigenous Indians, means "mountainous island."

# SPIRITS ALL AROUND

In Vodou [a word that means "energy"], spirits abound. Similar to saints and angels in other religions, these spirits are found everywhere and permeate everything. These *Lwa*, as they're known, are associated with all matter, whether it's a physical thing in nature, like a mountain, thundercloud, or ocean, or an invisible one, like the energies associated with birth, love, hope, and tragedy.

The source of all these spirits is the mother of the universe, a female power known as *Yehwe*. For this reason, Vodou is a very female-oriented religion. Priestesses who help lead believers in Vodou are as valued as priests. And many of Vodou's most important Lwa are female. Such womanly spirits include Lasyrenn, a spirit who lives in the ocean; Ezili Dantò, a protective mother figure; and Ezili Freda, a spirit associated with love and beauty.

While Haiti's slaves had triumphed in their fight for freedom, their lives continued to be plagued by hardship. Aside from the many slaves who died during the twelve-year-long revolt, others would be lost to famine or disease. Sugarcane fields, the nation's primary income source, had been torched in the violence. And politically, most nations around the world wouldn't recognize a nation led by emancipated slaves, let alone do business or trade with it.

Perhaps most poisonous, though, was the continued inequality throughout the country—of light-skinned Haitians (usually children of both white and Afro-Haitian descent) being treated preferentially over dark-skinned Afro-Haitians. This major power imbalance continues today and explains why the country's lower, or peasant, class suffers some of the worst poverty in the Western Hemisphere.

# ZOMBIS IN CULTURE AND RELIGIONS

Out of this deep, dark past, the zombi was born. In fact, the English word *zombie*, scooped up by American writers and travelers visiting Haiti in the 1930s, was an imperfect spelling of the Haitian word *zombi*. And this word (and its essential meaning) originated with the African slaves brought to the island. Their word, *nzambi*,

comes from the Congo region of West Africa and means "spirit of a dead person."

The zombi remains a powerful symbol in Haiti today, a reminder of the people's past oppression and a call to stand up and fight for one's rights. Haitians don't fear zombis—they fear *becoming* zombis.

Americans need a Vodou education. Our ideas about "voodoo" (wrong spelling, by the way!), including notions of black magic, witches, sorcerers, and little dolls (effigies or small figurines) being pricked with pins, is quite skewed, and in some cases, completely false! The truth is that Vodou is a religion, a culture, and a way of looking at the world that's practiced by over six million ordinary Haitians. It's similar to any other world religion in that it has its own professed god, spirits (which are akin to angels or saints), and system of values. Vodou offers its practitioners light, wisdom, and hope when dealing with life's troubles.

A man who guides others in Vodou is called a priest (or *houngan*), while a female guide is called a priestess (or *mambo*). They help practitioners connect and serve the variety of spirits that govern the universe. A Vodou ceremony—hardly a scary, bloody ritual—is typically a very ordinary affair involving coffee, rum, corn, and sweets.

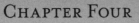

## CHAPTER FOUR

# MODERN ZOMBIES

"All I did was make them the neighbors."—American film
director George Romero on why the zombies in his film
*Night of the Living Dead* seemed so terrifying

Today's American zombie is decidedly gross and gory. Its beginning, though, was rooted in mystery and magic.

As we just learned, the zombi is an important part of Haiti's history. Americans' exposure to the haunting concept began in the 1920s when the United States' military occupied the island due to political turmoil. The almost-twenty-year occupation brought American soldiers, as well as writers and adventurers, who wished to explore the exotic country and its curious residents.

One of those inquisitive visitors was William Seabrook. The oddball journalist—who craved unusual assignments and was even willing to taste human flesh for one of them—is often credited with introducing the zombie to American audiences. Seabrook recounted his spooky escapades in Haiti in his sensational, best-selling 1929 book, *The Magic Island*.

To Seabrook, Haiti was a world of "marvels, miracles, and wonders." Befriended by some Haitians, the journalist got to witness a variety of colorful and riveting Vodou practices and rituals. Seabrook was both fascinated and frightened by what he saw—especially when he got the chance to meet what he thought was a *real, live zombie* working in a sugarcane field. (Keep in mind that the adventuresome Seabrook could have been exaggerating, or that local Haitians could have been pulling his leg!)

Nonetheless, this is his recollection: "Bonjour, compere," Seabrook said to the man (Meaning "Hello, host."). There was no response, only a blank-eyed stare. The journalist reached out to shake one of the zombie's "dangling hands." It felt "calloused, solid, human," he wrote.

The vacant-looking worker that Seabrook described was the feared zombie of Haitian myth.

Though according to lore, a person who many think is dead may, in fact, be heavily sedated with special medicines. The person cannot think or feel, but only act—a puppet to be manipulated for labor, work, or even evil deeds.

While Seabrook was in Haiti, he claimed to have seen several such zombies. He called them "corpses walking in the sunlight."

# HOLLYWOOD SEIZES ON ZOMBIES

Americans who read Seabrook's account were captivated. Haiti had an exotic allure, made even better with the addition of the "living dead." The 1930s was already the decade of the monster, especially the reanimated, crawling-out-of-their-tombs-and-coffins kinds. The period saw such hits as *Frankenstein* (1931), *Dracula* (1931), and *The Mummy* (1932). These frightful flicks (now considered comedies for their laughable special effects compared to today's!) allowed Americans a way to escape during the economic crisis known as the Great Depression.

# IT'S ALIVE!

Literature's influence on our concepts of monsters and the dead is profound. But no author toys and tinkers with the dead more masterfully than English writer Mary Shelley in her classic, *Frankenstein*. Frankenstein (the name of a scientist in the story and *not* the monster) sets about building a magnificent creature, piecing dead human body parts together the way you might build with LEGOs.

But the bold scientist's fascination soon turns to dread when his finished experiment comes to life and proves to be a freakish and vengeful beast with yellow eyes and translucent skin. Much more action and fright ensues in this gripping story, which is a must-read for any monster enthusiast!

It didn't take long before *White Zombie* (1932) joined Hollywood's list of monster movies. The first about zombies, it drew heavily from Seabrook's book. The story features Charles Beaumont, a lovestruck man desperate to attract a lover. Beaumont tries to woo the lovely Madeleine Short, who's already engaged to be married, but she rejects him. Frustrated, Beaumont enlists the help of a voodoo master named Murder Legendre. This priest tells Beaumont that the only way to win Madeleine over is to use a magic potion and turn her into a zombie.

The deed is done, but not without regret. When Beaumont kisses the blank-faced Madeleine laying in a coffin, he sees no emotion—he only feels her cold lips. He learns a lesson that most of us already know: that there's more to love than just good looks. Beaumont says it better in the movie: "I thought that beauty alone would satisfy. But the soul is gone. I can't bear those empty, staring eyes."

# THEY KEEP COMING

Following *White Zombie*, more zombie-inspired movies shuffled in. There was *Revolt of the Zombies* (1936), *The Walking Dead* (1936), *King of the Zombies* (1941), and *I Walked with a Zombie* (1943). Most of the films were premised on Haitian zombies, or at least what Americans believed they knew about them. Many were also classified as "B movies" because they were relatively cheap and easy to make. (The term *B movie* was originally used to designate the second movie that ran on a double bill.) Cheesy, with pathetic special effects, grainy picture quality, and bad acting, these movies now qualify as frightful fun!

# ZANY FOR ZOMBIES

Yes, modern zombies can be terrifying. But they can also be silly, serious, heroic, creative, loveable, and much more. In recent years, an assortment of fun zombie books has invaded the kids' sections of libraries and bookstores with titles like *Zombie Wants a Cookie*, *Zombelina*, *I Want to Eat Your Books*, and *My Big Fat Zombie Goldfish*. There's also the Plants vs. Zombies series, based on the popular video game, with books such as *Lawnmageddon* and *Soil Your Plants*!

Zombies also inspire plotting and strategy in board games like Monopoly: The Walking Dead (Survival Edition). They're a major feature in many video games, most of which are so unimaginatively gross and violent that they're actually bo-o-o-oring. More creepy is to actually squeeze on the guts of an anatomically correct zombie doll with products like the Inhuman Squishy Zombie! This zombie, sporting removable limbs and cascading organs that can be squeezed, comes with a graphic novel that invites readers to dissect a hypothetical "zombie epidemic."

# NO BRAINER

In 1968, a new, more terrifying zombie rose from the grave in America. Like a creepy sleepwalker, it shambled along, hunting for its next human victim. Moaning, groaning, and eager to nibble on human body parts, this zombie made its first appearance in the all-time horror classic *Night of the Living Dead*.

At first, the movie's creator, George Romero, referred to his undead characters as ghouls, not zombies. But the image he created—of normal-looking people (say your neighbors or classmates) returning from the dead to eat people for lunch—was powerful.

Just like today's kids, today's zombies are very different. Unlike their "cousins" of Haitian lore, modern American zombie characters are typically evil, crave human flesh, can transmit their "zombiness" like a pesky cold, and are nearly impossible to destroy. "They Won't Stay Dead!" was a famous tagline from *Night of the Living Dead*.

As for zombies and brains, that connection appears to have come later. For instance, in Romero's movie classic, the lurching monsters nosh on plenty of body parts, but NOT on anyone's noodle. (In fact, when he was once asked about the absence of brain-binging in his film, Romero replied, "Who says zombies eat brains?")

American zombies appear to have first developed a taste for spongy pink (or gray) matter in 1985's *The Return of the Living Dead* movie. Why might monsters have such cravings? Well, for one, it makes for decidedly disgusting viewing pleasure! For another, it may be that zombies eat brains to absorb intelligence, or to feel good. (The "pleasure centers" must be their favorite part!)

# ZOMBIE SURVIVAL 101

If you're ever confronted with a rotting-faced zombie, you should ... offer him a breath mint! No, but seriously, you'll want to be prepared! Consider these survival tips (which, by the way, are helpful in any emergency situation).

• Stock up on fresh bottled water and pantry goods. This way if a horde of zombies storms your hood, you can just lock up the doors, snuggle in tight, and not worry about heading out for fast food!

• Prepare a well-stocked first aid kit, which includes bandages, ointments, pain relievers, and any other medicines your family requires.

• Have an emergency radio on hand, plus plenty of flashlights.

• Slather yourself with rotten meat. Just kidding, of course! But die-hard zombie believers think that dousing oneself with the smell of decay camouflages the otherwise delicious human aroma!

• Be ready to journal your adventure. After all, you might write your own zombie book, play, or movie one day!

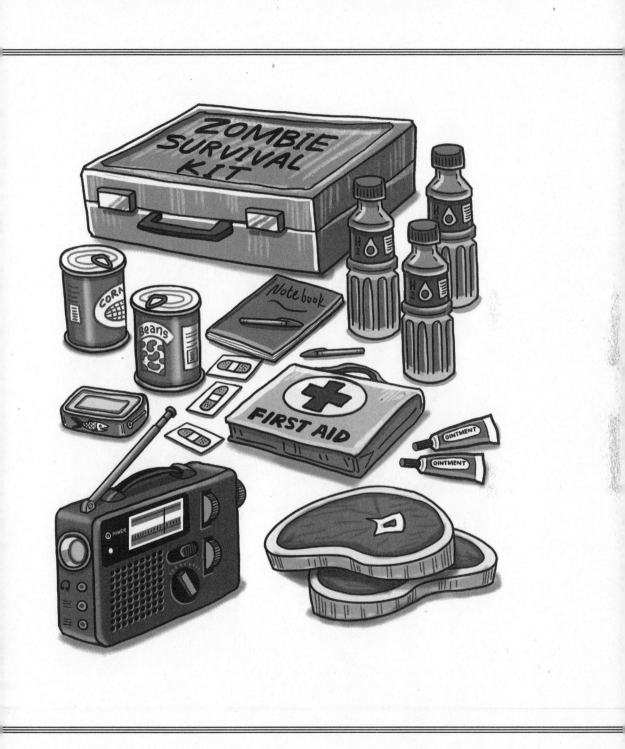

CHAPTER FIVE

# MONSTER IN THE MIRROR

"Don't you get it? *We* are the walking dead!"
—Robert Kirkman, comic book writer and creator
of the popular television series *The Walking Dead*

**W**hy are zombies so popular? What is it about them that's so frightening (aside from the fact that they look and smell like death and want to eat us)?

Again, it might be worthwhile to consider the zombis of Haiti and West Africa. For the most part, this zombi was not a real person or creature. It was a terrible and haunting experience. Black Haitians who endured the misery of slavery had been treated so cruelly that they *felt* like zombies, stripped of their spirits and souls.

Most of us can only remotely fathom what this awful experience must have been like. But in some ways, today's zombie borrows a tiny bit from this powerful concept.

It's harder for kids to relate to, but here's an example. Imagine you're at a subway station or on a crowded street or riding the school bus (things you might do every day). You shuffle along with the rest of the kids and people. You're stuck, with seemingly nowhere else to go. If you're on the school bus, maybe you feel like you've gotten on and off the bus a million times. You feel like you have no say in the matter—that you're just going from point A to point B, over and over and over again. You're bored. You're restless. And, sometimes, you just don't care.

This is an eyes-glazed-over zombie experience. And maybe, part of our current obsession with zombies has something to do with our fears about turning into human robots that have no fun or passion for life.

# ZOMBIES AND SCIENCE

The word *zombie* is so popular and well-understood in our vocabulary that it's being used to describe bizarre wonders in science and nature.

Take, for instance, the ant that falls victim to a particularly nasty fungus known as *Ophiocordyceps unilateralis*. The fungus invades the ant's brain, where it then releases a complex cocktail of chemicals that brainwashes the ant. The ant, now the slave of the fungus, climbs onto vegetation preferred by the fungus. The name of this diabolical entity? The "zombie fungus," of course!

Other zombies in nature include "zombie worms," "zombie snails," and "zombie volcanoes." Google them to learn more.

# ZOMBIE SIGHTINGS?

But what about reports of actual zombies? Witnesses have reported seeing people that look "zoned out," who have no apparent thoughts or emotions. Such cases have been reported in such places as Haiti, where of course, many locals already have unique cultural and spiritual ideas about zombies.

When researchers investigate, though, most find a rational explanation. In poor countries, including Haiti, one of those explanations is mental illness. There are a variety of psychological disorders—including epilepsy, fetal alcohol syndrome, and schizophrenia—which can cause "odd" symptoms in patients. With catatonic schizophrenia, for instance, patients may remain motionless for long periods of time, even after they've been spoken to or touched. Affected patients may also hold up their limbs in midair or make unusual facial expressions.

Sadly across history, there have been many people accused of being zombies, witches, and demons who, in truth, were just coping with misunderstood mental illnesses.

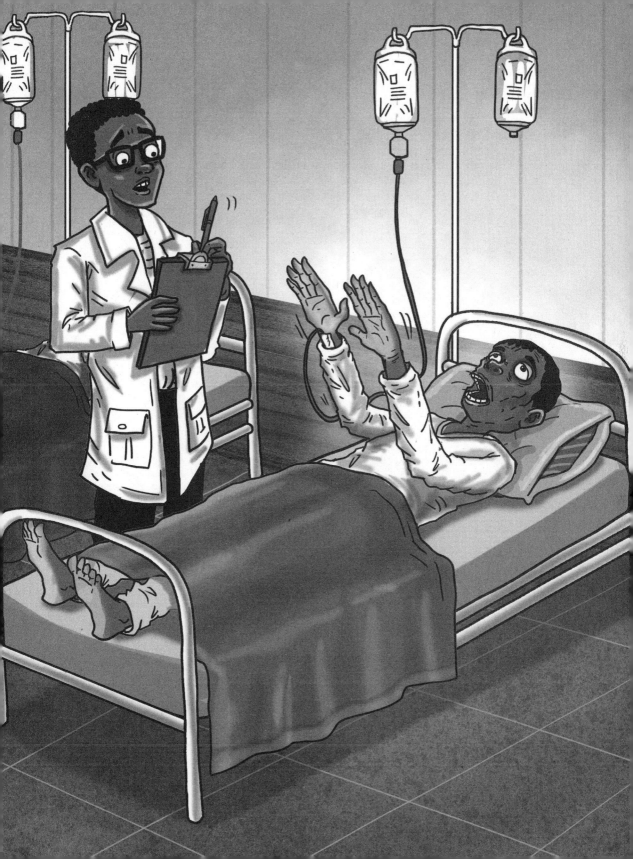

Like a helpful, universal contagion, zombies have invaded the worlds of science, economics, and mathematics. They've made these disciplines easier to understand. For instance, would you invest in a "zombie stock?" Probably not—they involve a lot of risk!

With the walking dead splashed across all kinds of media—books, movies, and television shows—zombies have become a well-known commodity. Probably the most frightening aspect about today's zombie is its ability to spread its "zombiness" through a virus that leaps from one person to another. It's the idea of a zombie pandemic—and a quickly moving virus—which has inspired some mathematicians to develop new models and equations.

Researchers don't believe in zombies. The concept of a zombie outbreak is just a fun and engaging way to approach challenging math models. And the researchers' computations could someday be helpful in projecting how quickly a *real* viral threat might spread.

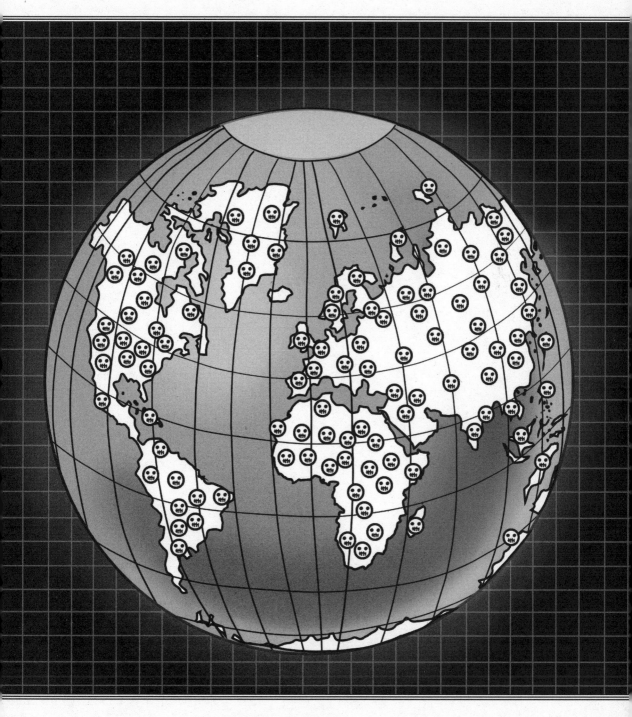

CONCLUSION

# DON'T BE A ZOMBIE

"Hey, this is rough!
Hey, this is tough!
Our soul in a bottle!
This is tough!"
—Lyrics from "Nanm Nan Boutey," an Afro-Haitian protest
song that means "Soul in a Bottle"

**M**any of today's Haitians use the zombie as a symbol to stir fire in people's bellies. It serves as a reminder to not be apathetic in society and to stay involved in one's community and stand up against injustice.

We can also use the symbol of the zombie in our own lives. It can invoke us to act if we see something wrong (for instance, someone being hurt or treated unfairly). It can remind us to be alive and in the moment. It can inspire us to pursue our passions in life—and not settle for things that make us bored.

Now, no more shuffling or mindlessly shambling through life. You're a zombie expert now. You have no excuses!

## Main Sources

Crosley, Reginald. The Vodou Quantum Leap. Minnesota: Llewellyn Publications, 2000.

Davis, Wade. The Serpent and the Rainbow. New York: Warner Books, 1985.

Desmangles, Leslie G. The Faces of the Gods: Vodou and Roman Catholicism in Haiti. North Carolina: The University of North Carolina Press, 1992.

Penzler, Otto. Zombies! Zombies! Zombies! New York: Vintage Crime/Black Lizard, 2011.

Shelley, Mary. Frankenstein. New York: Dover Publications, 1994.

Also: The Epic of Gilgamesh (Don't expect to find an original or reprinted book version of this ancient poem in your local library!) Modern translations can be found online at such sites as: aina.org/books/eog/eog.pdf

The Arabian Nights (Look for kids' collections of these stories, including a classic compilation by Grosset and Dunlap)

## For Further Reading

Want to read more about zombies . . . until you're blank in the face? Zombie books abound and aren't limited to the scary/horror genre.

You might consider the following titles (or check with a local librarian for recommended books):

*Dead City* by James Ponti

*Diary of a Minecraft Zombie* by Zach Zombie

*The Last Kids on Earth* by Max Brallier

*The Undertakers: The Rise of the Corpses* by Ty Drago

*The Zombie Chasers* by John Kloepfer and Steve Wolfhard